BREAK___
GH STARTUPS

Crush The Competition With Your Innovative Startup

Jonathan S. Walker

DEDICATION

I dedicate this book as well to my two beautiful children and my loving wife who have been nothing short of being my light and joy throughout the years.

Furthermore, the transmission, duplication or reproduction of any of the following work including specific information will be considered an illegal act irrespective of if it is done electronically or in print. This extends to creating a secondary or tertiary copy of the work or a recorded copy and is only allowed with express written consent from the Publisher. All additional right reserved.

The information in the following pages is broadly considered to be a truthful and accurate account of facts and as such any inattention, use or misuse of the information in question by the reader will render any resulting actions solely under their purview. There are no scenarios in which the publisher or the original author of this work can be in any fashion deemed liable for any hardship or damages that may befall them after undertaking information described herein.

Additionally, the information in the following pages is intended only for informational purposes and should thus be thought of as universal. As befitting its nature, it is presented without assurance regarding its prolonged validity or interim quality. Trademarks that are mentioned are done without written consent and can in no way be considered an endorsement from the trademark holder.

CONTENTS

Part 1

Introduction

Chapter 1: Do You Have Traction?
Chapter 2: Offline
Chapter 3: Emails

Chapter 4: Viral

Chapter 5: Public Speaking

Part 2

Chapter One: Affiliate Marketing, Website Creation, & Keyword Research
Chapter Two: Essential Affiliate Marketing Tips
Chapter Three: Various Affiliate Marketing Strategies
Chapter Four: Amazon's Affiliate Marketing Program
Chapter Five: Common Mistakes To Avoid

Part 3

Chapter 1: Understanding Network Marketing
Chapter 2: Tips on How To Find Network Marketing Success
Chapter 3: Successful Network Marketing Strategies & How To Find Your Audience
Chapter 4: Common Mistakes The New Network Marketrs Make & How To Avoid Them
Conclusion

VIP Subscriber List

Dear Reader, If you would like to receive latest tips and tricks on internet marketing, exclusive strategies, upcoming books & promotions, and more, do subscribe to my mailing list in the link below! I will be giving away a free book that you can download right away as well after you subscribe to show my appreciation!

Here's the link: http://bit.do/jonathanswalker

INTRODUCTION

Congratulations on purchasing your personal copy of *Breakthrough Startups: Crush The Competition With Your Innovative Startups.* Thank you for doing so.

The following chapters will discuss some of the many ways that you can build your startup traction.

You will discover the importance of marketing and the effect that it can have on your business and its success.

There are plenty of books on this subject on the market, thanks again for choosing this one! Every effort was made to ensure it is full of as much useful information as possible. Please enjoy!

Congratulations on purchasing your personal copy of Breakthrough Startups. Thank you for doing so.

DO YOU HAVE TRACTION?

New startup companies and businesses will often have a hard time getting up and running. Being able to get the capital to fund a new business and keep it going can be hard for new businesses that don't have the time to prove their abilities in the marketplace. When a business creates traction, it helps the company to attract possible investors and gain an edge over their competition.

Business traction tells us the progress a new business has and its momentum it gains as it grows. There isn't a certain way that a company can measure traction, but most businesses rely on their revenue and how customers respond to their product. The reason for traction is to make sure the business grows and meets certain objectives and goals. This may seem like an abstract thought, it is imperative and allows a business to understand where, in the industry, it stands and where they want to get.

Traction may be important to the company's founders and workers; it is also equally important to stakeholders and investors who are interested in the organization. The better the traction, the more investors that company will attract. As a result of attracting more investors, the company will also have more funds available to them to help them succeed. This means that developing good business traction is imperative to all new businesses and should be a part of the company's business plan.

The first steps to creating a successful startup are, understanding the organization's future, creating goals, and figuring out a way to reach those goals. Having clearly stated goals in your mission statement and your business plan will show investors how they can expect the company to progress in relation to the factors of the marketplace and competition. However, just coming up with your goals isn't enough. To know your traction, you have to understand the metrics you will be using to define your success. Depending on what industry you're in and the external factors of the marketplace, traction could be measured through market research, sales, or customer response.

Even the most well-intentioned company, with a perfect business plan, can still struggle to find traction. There are millions of reasons as to why so many startups fail, the most common is a lack of brand or product awareness. When competition begins to grow in the marketplace, the smaller businesses that aren't as well known will become overwhelmed by larger brands. To avoid this problem, new companies need to increase the marketing and advertising efforts.

OFFLINE

When online marketing started to grow in popularity, people forgot about the many proven offline marketing methods. Online marketing is important, many of the other techniques in this book are online, but engaging your customer's offline is a distinct and unique method that shouldn't be forgotten.

If you're looking to boost your marketing, start trying some outside of the box tactics. Let's look at five almost forgotten offline marketing methods that require little to no budget.

OFFLINE GUERRILLA MARKETING

Guerrilla marketing refers to the use of unique marketing methods, and since online marketing is so strictly structured, offline is the easiest area to try out some guerrilla marketing tactics. At this point, you can forget everything you know about how marketing channels work and allow your inner child to have some fun. Offline guerrilla methods include:

- Create temporary images on cars, buildings, etc. with sticky notes.

- Create branded bookmarks and give them to your local library.

- "Accidentally" leave behind a pen with your brand on it at the bank.

- Draw advertisements on the sidewalk with chalk.

- Place sticky notes with your business on it in random places.

- **BUSINESS CARDS**

- This is a guerrilla tactic that needs to be talked about specifically. This is a necessity and not an option like the other methods I mentioned earlier. If you run a business of any kind, whether established, small, or a startup, you have to have business cards, and you need to hand them out. Don't just give them to people that you meet; drop them everywhere you go.

- Places you should leave behind a business card at:

- Always drop your business card in a contest fish bowl that is asking for cards.

- Place your business cards in books at the library that relates to your company.

- Whenever you see a public bulletin board; pin your business card to it.

- When you pay your bill at a restaurant, leave behind a business card.

- **PHOTOGRAPH AND FILM EVERYTHING**

- Since social media marketing is only online, most marketers and owners will forget that they can boost the social campaigns through offline efforts. Simple ways to do so is by taking photos of daily activities and company events and post them online. You can do the same with videos as well. If you or somebody else from your company speaks at an important event, record the speech and upload it to your social media accounts.

- When you use real-life photos and videos from your company's offline world, you are showing your company's personality and increasing your user engagement. A Facebook post that has a photo will receive 84% more clicks, and two times as many like than a text-only post. There are also a lot of social media networks that are the only image based, such as Tumblr, Pinterest, and Instagram.

- **DONATE PRODUCTS AND GIFT CERTIFICATES AS A PRIZE**

- When you offer your service or product as a prize for a local contest, you will build your business's visibility, while also showing that you are committed to your local community. If your business is a beauty supply store, you could donate a gift certificate or a gift basket for your most popular products. The organization you donate the product or service to may even announce your brand prize to a room of sponsors. They may even publish you business names in ads in various publications, like a press release, website, or newsletter.

- **MAKE PUBLIC APPEARANCES**

- Public events provide you a great way to build your brand's awareness, meet new people, and share ideas. They become even more effective when you speak at these events. Locate a local event that is related to your industry, figure out what people want to learn about your business, and volunteer to speak. If you don't have the clout to get to speak at these sorts of events, just attending them can be as worthwhile.

- You don't have to use all of these offline marketing methods, just start implementing at least one. Write down a promotion on a few sticky notes and take them with you. You never know what could happen.

-

-

-

-

-

E-MAILS

- Your average consumer's inbox is full of marketing messages with attention-grabbing subject lines trying to compete with you. Each day there are over 144 billion emails sent out; making email marketing one of the best online channels for business marketing and communication. The trick is to separate yourself from everybody else.

- Figuring out your key message is important to your bottom line no matter what your goal is. The following eight email strategies will ensure that your emails will stand out amongst your competitions, and will help you achieve your goals.

- **PERSONALIZE WITHOUT THE CONSUMER'S NAME**

- You know longer have to worry about "Dear [insert name here]." Having a personalized email greeting isn't as effective as you may think. Research performed by Temple's Fox School of Business has even suggested that this personalization can be harmful. People become wary about emails with personalizing greetings because of the concerns about credit card fraud, phishing, and identity theft.

- An important part of email marketing is the relationship. Does your recipient trust you? Does the recipient actually know who you are? When you send out an email the jumps the familiarity

8

gun too soon, your personalization will appear to be a bit sketchy. Intimacy had to be earned in the real world, so emails work the same way.

- When you fake familiarity, you will likely turn many of your email readers off. Now, this doesn't mean that all personalization forms are off limits. In fact, certain brand personalizations can help you out: sending an email that gives your subscriber individuality. This could simply mean their purchase history.

- This means if you want to personalize your emails, do it in a meaningful way. It doesn't take much of relationship or knowledge to put your consumer's name in your email greeting. Sending a personalized email that is recipient specific shows a lot more care.

- **THE IMPORTANCE OF SUBJECT LINES**

- It seems that when it comes down to crafting your subject line, there is only one thing you have to avoid: a 60 to 70 character subject line. Marketers call this the subject length "dead zone." Research performed by Adestra tracked over 900 million emails, and there wasn't any increase in click-through or open rates at the 60 to 70 character subject line length.

- On the opposite side of things, subject lines that contained more than 70 characters were more beneficial in engaging readers and getting them to click through to the content and subject lines that at less than 49 characters tested better for email open rates. Surprisingly, they found that subject lines that had less than ten characters at 58% open rate.

- The use of short subjects came into vogue when President Barack Obama used them in his fundraising emails. There was amazing engagement with subject lines such as "Wow" and "Hey."

- Now the question is: Are you looking for opens or boost clicks? Create long subject lines for more click-through, or keep them short for more opens. Either way, just make sure that you keep your subject lines out of the 60 to 70 character range.

- **EMAIL PRIMETIME: 8 PM TO MIDNIGHT**

- While quality emails may be created during regular business hours, the ones that are more likely to be open aren't sent between nine and five. The best time to send an email is at night. Experian Marketing Services discovered that the emails that received the best open rate had been sent between 8 pm and midnight. This time not only did well for open rates, but it did better for sales and click-through. 8 pm to midnight is also the least used, which helps the late night emails perform better than the rest.

- Deployment time and inbox crowding also work together. This means that if your email goes out at a time when others don't, it stands a better chance of being noticed. Mailing your customers at their optimal time will be up to you. You will need to make sure at run some tests to see when you receive the best response.

- **EVERYBODY LIKES SOMETHING FOR FREE**

- Consumers love receiving things for free. Bluewire Media tested different types of content on their 6,300 subscribers to find out what free items got the highest clicks and open. Their winners were tools and templates.

- Most consumers will want to know what's in it for them and Bluewire Media found that tools and templates greatly outweighed photo albums, brain teasers, expert interviews, and ebooks. You will have to do your own tests with your own subscribers, but using this information is a great head start.

- **OPENS ON MOBILE DEVICES ACCOUNTED FOR 47% OF ALL OPENS**

- Look at it this way, if your emails get you $100,000 in sales every month, would you want to say goodbye to $44,000 just because you emails show up weird on mobile devices?

- You need to make sure you design you email responsively so that they look great no matter where they are being read. These are some mobile design tips that can help:

- Ergonomic: Most people with scroll and tap with their thumb, so place interactive elements in the middle.

- Make an obvious, and easy to use, call-to-action. Above the fold it best.

- Make sure you follow the iOS guidelines for buttons: 44 pixels wide by 44 pixels tall.

- Make your font size better to make them easier to read on smartphones.

- Change your email to a one column template.

- **EMAIL IS BETTER THAN TWITTER AND FACEBOOK**

- Social media may be on email's heels, but the inbox kind still has a greater influence over social media. SocialTwist monitored 119 referral campaigns for over 18 months that were performed by leading companies and brands. They found that there was a significant advantage to an email's ability to create new customers as compared to Twitter and Facebook. There were 300,000 referrals that became new customers, and of that 50.8 % were reached by email, 22 % through Facebook, and 26.8% through Twitter.

- **EMAIL ON WEEKENDS**

- Saturday and Sunday didn't outperform the 8 pm to midnight time, but they did outperform the other weekdays. Just like at the 8 to midnight time, a number of emails sent on the weekends are low, which helps your messages to stand out. The margins for sales rates, click-through, and opens were not that substantial, but every little bit counts when it comes to email marketing.

- **RE-ENGAGING OLD SUBSCRIBERS**

- You have a huge list, awesome. The problem is that 2/3s of those people are likely inactive. Research has discovered that a subscribers list of inactivity is 63%. This means that once a person joins your list, they are less likely to actually follow up with any of your emails. Listrak has said that the first 90 days are important to change a sign-up to a devotee.

- That 63% now needs to be re-engaged. The trick is to figure out what kind of re-engagement campaign will work the best for you followers. It's quite likely, that if you have already been doing research, you have found different kinds of results.

• VIRAL

- It's true; the term viral marketing does sound offensive. Saying that you are a viral marketer will likely cause people to take a couple of steps back. A virus is a feared thing, which is not quite dead and not completely alive. But you have to admit a virus is admirable. It is able to live in secrecy until it is able to reproduce several times. It even piggybacks onto other hosts to increase its own tribe.

- So how does a virus translate to marketing? Viral marketing is a strategy that gets a consumer to pass on a message to other people, which create a potentially exponential growth in the influence and exposure to the message. Like a virus, these strategies take advantage of fast multiplication to send out a message to thousands or even millions.

- Hotmail.com is a classic example of viral marketing at work. Their strategy was simple:

1. Give people free email addresses and services

2. They placed a tag at the bottom of each message that said: "Get your private, free email at www.hotmail.com."

3. Then they sat back and waited while people emailed their family and friends

4. People notice the emails

5. Those people register so that they get their own email; all leading up to

6. They pass the word on to a growing number of associates and friends.

7. Their message spread like the small waves that ripple off of the water after a pebble is dropped into a pond. You too can make a viral marketing strategy that ripples out to more and more people.

8. Before you begin coming up with your strategy you have to accept the fact that some strategies will work better than other ones depending on your audience. There is very few that work as well as the Hotmail message. But we are going to look

at six unique concepts that you should try to use in your marketing plans. Your strategy doesn't have to contain every single one of these elements, but the more that you use, the more powerful your result will become. An effective strategy should try to have:

1. Service or product giveaway

2. Makes it easy to transfer to others

3. Is able to be scaled from small to large

4. Taps into common behaviors and motivations

5. Makes use of existing networks for communication

6. Use others' resources

7. Let's look at each of these a little more.

8. **SERVICE OR PRODUCT GIVEAWAY**

9. Free, like we've talked about before, is a powerful word in marketing. Most of the viral marketing programs out there will give away valuable services and products to attract their consumer's attention. These free things could be free "cool" buttons, free information, free email services, or free software programs that are able to do powerful things, but not everything that the "pro" version is able to do. The words inexpensive and cheap will generate some interest, but the word free will do the same only faster. Viral marketers aren't afraid of delayed gratification. They are okay with not make

any profit today, but if they are able to create a bunch of interest from free things, they will be able to profit soon and for forever. You have to have patience. Free will attract eyeballs, those eyeballs will then wander to the countless things that *aren't* free which you're selling, and there you have sales. Eyeballs will provide you with sales opportunities, email addresses, and advertising revenue.

10. MAKES IT EASY TO TRANSFER TO OTHERS

11. Doctors and nurses will tell you that during flu season, you should do everything in your power to avoid being contaminated. This is because viruses are only able to spread when they can be easily transmitted. The medium that you use to carry your marketing message needs to be easily transferred and replicated: software download, graphic, website, and email. Viral marketing works amazingly on the internet since there are inexpensive and easy communication sources. Digital formats make it easy to copy things. When you look at it in terms of marketing, the entire idea is to make things as simple and shareable as possible. Generally, when it comes to a marketing message, short is the way to go. Make sure that your message is copied, compelling, and compressed at the bottom of each of your email messages.

12. IS ABLE TO BE SCALED FROM SMALL TO LARGE

13. However you decide to transmit your message, the ultimate goal should be that it's super simple for it to catch fire and spread. To look back at the free email accounts method, there's a fundamental flaw: if the campaign is *too* effective, more users may end up trying to join than server space is available. Otherwise, the new users will be left unaccommodated, and as a result, the campaign will start to fail. Nobody wants a worthless email account, even if it is free. Taking it back to the virus analogy, if the virus is to kill the person that is hosting it before the virus is able to transmit itself, the virus effectively is failing at its job. However, if the email provider were to plan ahead so that the new accounts could certainly be properly be accommodated, regardless of how successful the campaign is, then everything will be alright. The key point is that everything has to be scalable in terms of your campaign; if it can't go from small to big with no problems, then there's a fundamental flaw.

14. TAPS INTO COMMON BEHAVIORS AND MOTIVATIONS

15. A good marketing campaign will always tap into humanity's seedy mental underbelly. Greed drives people. People want desperately to be "cool", as well as loved and understood. By taking advantage of these perfectly human tendencies, you'll generate hundreds of thousands of website hits and millions of email mentions. So, in order to build a strong marketing plan, you have to take advantage of our most human qualities and desires; that, friend, is how you build a winning marketing plan.

16. MAKES US OF EXISTING NETWORKS FOR COMMUNICATION

17. Most everyone is social. Social scientists have figured out that everybody has at least 12 people in their network of associates, family, and friends. Their broader network might consist of thousands of people; ultimately this depends upon what they do and how important they are. For example, a waiter may talk with a huge number of customers every week. The best marketers are those who have a strong understanding of how powerful these interpersonal bridges can be, whether they are strong interpersonal bridges – like those with family and friends – or weak ones, like with customers. Everybody who uses the internet also has a rather extensive network, as well. They get favorite websites and email addresses. Affiliate marketing programs take advantage of these internet-based networks. The way to rapidly make your message spread is to find your way into these interpersonal connections.

18. USE OTHERS' RESOURCES

19. The best marketing strategies are those that take advantage of others' resources to help get the word out. Affiliate marketing plans, for example, put graphic links or text on other people's websites. A single news article, if pertinent and popular, will be taken up by a huge number of other websites and sources of content. Somebody else's web page or newsprint is relying on your marketing message. Somebody else's resources get depleted and not yours.

20.

21.
22.
23.
24.
25.
26.

27.

28. PUBLIC SPEAKING

29.

30. One of the many responsibilities of being a small business owner is being the face of your company. You are already the main customer relationship manager. You must be its lead promoter and champion to grow your business. One way that this can be done is to actively participate and attend conferences that are related to your industry. Another way is to give talks to potential customers.

31. The following resources and tips can help you find speaking opportunities and conferences that are relevant to your business. They can also help you get speaking engagements, too.

32. Learning to listen before you speak is an excellent idea. Before you begin doing your own presentations you need to attend sessions that others in your fields are giving. You will pick up on what presentations are popular. You might see gaps that you might be able to fill with your own expertise. If you ask questions and provide different insights during the question and answer time during these presentations, you might be remembered if you apply to speak at a related event at a later date.

33. When you feel like you are ready to represent your business

and share your expertise, you will need to find speaking engagements. You need to find groups that are looking for speakers and sell yourself on your talk. The first thing to do is to make a speaker's one-sheet. This is a one-page introduction to your topic and yourself. It will provide a jumping-off point for self-promoting yourself as a speaker.

34. Now you need to look for organizations that are looking for speakers for certain events. You can do a google search to look for speaking events in your area. There are also paid services that will match speakers with certain event organizers. You can offer your services to groups that may benefit from your expertise.

35. To be a successful speaker you have to provide some value to your audience. This means that you have to share your expertise not just promote your business. Your first presentation will be the hardest. You will get better with time. You will start getting reviews and testimonials that you will be able to use to help promote yourself as a speaker. You will soon find yourself being regarded as an expert and the face of your company and industry.

36. Here are some ways to get speaking engagements to help market your business:

1. Become a better speaker: This sounds obvious, but by being a more polished, engaging speaker, you will gain more

opportunities to speak. If you are a very good speaker, you can ask for testimonials from the people that invited you to speak. These testimonials go a long way when others are looking for speakers.

2. How can you become a better speaker? The best and easiest way is to record each presentation and watch it later. Take notes of what you would like to improve on. Try focusing on different things every time you speak. How you stand, where you put your hands, how you modulate your voice. With time, you will be an extraordinary speaker.

3. Know your material: Knowing your material inside and out will help you become a better speaker because it will ease your nerves. First, you absolutely must know your speech. You need to practice it over and over. By knowing your speech means you can be confident and at ease when you step on a stage and face the crowd. Being prepared is a great way to overcome nerves.

4. Knowing your speech isn't enough. You must be an expert in your area. The more that you know, the more confident you will be when taking questions from your audience.

5. The most important thing about your presentation it that it is not a pitch. You should not be trying to sell anything. Give the audience things they can take with them that they can use and actions they can follow. Your main goal is to help them.

6. Have a speaking page on your website: Add a page that promotes yourself as a speaker. It is the best way to get engagements. On this speaking page, post a demo reel, maybe a few clips from a previous engagement that you have posted on YouTube. Include a biography, topics that you can talk about, and titles of some signature speeches you can give in a moment's notice.

7. A page that shows your availability and expertise as a speaker allows event planners and others to see you speak and get a feel of what you will be like on stage. They like to see that you can actually engage with an audience.

8. Build the right relationships: Many business owners think they must speak at large corporations or events to market their businesses effectively. This is not true. There are plenty of small groups that want to hear what you have to say. The most important thing is to have a clear target market and speak where they are going to be.

9. When you find some businesses, ask them what topics they want to hear about. Give them your one sheet and tell them that you are available to speak. If you have an engagement that is open to the public, send an email to contacts and invite them to come. If you add a video to your website, send a link with a not about the topic and video.

10. Someone you have been building a relationship with will have

an opportunity for you to speak. You have been persistent, and they will think about you first.

11. Speak for free: When you first start to speak, you should do it for free. This could mean you might have to speak free for years before you ever get your first paying gig.

12. Speaking for free gives you the expertise to be good enough to not charge for your speaking services but to speak at larger venues.

13. When you can start charging to speak, you will have good reasons to continue to speak for free. When you know that you will not be traveling for a while, send out emails to local contacts and let them know that you are in town and have time to speak.

14. For local gigs, offer a lower rate or do them for free especially if it is a group within your target market. You just might walk away with some new business.

15.
16.
17.
18.
19.
20.

21.

22.

23.

24.

25. PART 2

26.

27.

28.

29. Chapter 1: Affiliate Marketing, Website Creation, and Keyword Research

30. Affiliate marketing on the internet can be best defined as when you, the website developer, creates a website that promotes other people's products. Whenever someone else's product sells due to traffic that has manifested on your website, you get paid a commission. One of the greatest advantages that affiliate marketing can provide an individual is that you do not need to develop an entirely new product on your own in order to see a profit. By focusing on website development, rather than product development, you're able to avoid high shipping and manufacturing costs. Two key aspects of affiliate marketing involve creating a website and conducting keyword research.

31. Creating a Website

32. You're not going to be able to become an affiliate marketer without a website. This may sound daunting, but there are plenty of programs out there that can help you achieve this goal, including Wix, SquareSpace, and WordPress. WordPress is probably the best tool to use because it will rank better in the eyes of Google than will the other two options. The average cost of starting a website including the following:

Domain Name	$10 Per Year
Web Hosting	$10 Per Month
SEO Help	$10 Per Month
Total	$250 Annually

33. When you think about startup costs that are associated with other types of businesses, $250 is nothing! You can opt to skip the cost of SEO assistance, but you'll see in a minute why you definitely don't want to do that.

34. SEO, Keyword Research, and Niche Topics

35. An essential aspect of good affiliate marketing involves setting up your website to revolve around a niche topic that is going to attract a specific client base. The competition on the internet is fierce, which is why this research step is essential prior to setting up your website. To achieve this, you are going to need to becoming acquainted with SEO, or Search Engine Optimization. The first websites that come up when you type something into Google are ones that are great at meeting SEO standards. The administrators for these sites are keeping a close eye on what people like you and me are typing into Google in regards to the product that they're trying to sell. They are then making sure that the content on their website is meeting the needs of the keyword traffic that is coming through Google.

36. This is why SEO research is so important, and why you should opt to pay for help with SEO when you have this option. Some of the best SEO websites including the

following:

1. Moz.com

2. Searchengineland.com

3. SEObook.com

    4. When you go onto these websites, you're able to type in a keyword and find the amount of traffic that Google is seeing for this particular word or phrase. Specifically for your website, you should be looking for a keyword that is related to a broad topic that has a high volume of searches, but a low amount of competition. For example, starting a website that advertises all yoga gear is not good enough; you're going to be competing with companies like Lululemon and Athleta. A niche site would instead be one that focuses only on new products in yoga props, for example. When you're researching for your website, make sure that your keyword is truly niche in nature. Try to be as detailed as possible.

5.

6. Chapter 2: Essential Affiliate Marketing Tips

7. Once you have decided on your niche topic and have done extensive keyword research, your work is far from over. The next step is to develop your website. Affiliate marketers typically will use product reviews in order to see a profit. The basic premise here is to review products that people are searching frequently because these types of consumers want to be assured that they're buying a reliable product prior to purchase. Some of the basic types of posts that affiliate marketers will put on their sites include the following:

1. **Direct Posts:** These are product reviews. These reviews will include features about the product in question, and most importantly will have a link to purchase the product somewhere in the post.

2. **List Posts:** List posts are becoming more popular these days because they can be read quickly and can be easily shared on other sites such as Facebook or Twitter. Some great list posts include "How-to" posts or "10 Best" list posts.

3. **Indirect Posts:** You write about the product that you're trying to promote, but without actually referencing the product itself. Instead, you provide links to the product that you're promoting throughout the content of the article. The point of an indirect post is to create curiosity about the product in question.

4. **Comparison Posts:** A comparison post is great because you're able to promote two products at once. You'll want to keep a positive tone for each of the products that you're promoting and highlight both of their features equally.

5. **Special Offer Posts:** These types of posts will offer a coupon or a discount at the end of the read, which will keep the reader engaged throughout the entire article with the hope that they will eventually purchase the product.

6. As you can see from these different types of posts, an affiliate website is a site that could almost be disguised as a blog. You want to convey the message that you're an expert on whatever it is you're discussing, but keep all of the posts as product-oriented as possible. Without the factor of reputability, consumers are not going to take your affiliate site seriously because it will seem like you're uninformed.

7. **The Type of Products You Should be Recommending**

8. Ideally, you should only be reviewing products on your affiliate website about which you're passionate or familiar.

It's likely that consumers are going to know when you're reviewing something that is not personally exciting to you or that is not truly a great product in your eyes. Seek to be as authentic as possible, and your readers are sure to feel this sense of genuineness come through in your posts. This is a good rule to keep in mind for the type of keyword that you're going to be focusing on as well. You want to make sure that you're generally excited about the topic of your website as a whole. Just because a keyword ranks well on Google, it does not 100% mean that you should definitely create a website around it. You should also be passionate about the topic yourself.

9. **Recommending Versus Telling**

10. Another rule that many affiliate marketers swear by is that you should never outright tell people to purchase a product on your site. A better way to get through to people is to recommend what you're selling from the position of personal experience. This will make your online identity more relatable, and will most likely lead to more sales.

11.

12.

13.

14.

15.

16.

17.

18. Chapter 3: Various Affiliate Marketing Strategies

19. Depending on the specific affiliate marketing program in which you choose to partake, the parameters of each one could be different. Here we will look at some of the different types of affiliate marketing strategies that exist so that you can find a program that best fits what you're trying to accomplish through your own affiliate marketing presence on the internet.

20. Type 1: Cost Per Click

21. When you find a company that will pay you a commission on a "cost per click" basis, this means that whenever someone who visits your site clicks on the link that leads them to the seller's page, you get paid regardless of whether or not they purchase the product.

22. Type 2: Cost Per Sale

23. This means that the seller is only going to agree to pay you a commission when your website's link leads to an actual sale. This is considered to be one of the tougher ways to make money through affiliate marketing because there is not much you can do to control whether or not a consumer actually purchases the product after seeing it on your website.

24. Type 3: Cost Per Lead

25. For this type of affiliate marketing strategy, the seller is going to pay you whenever the link on your website leads a consumer to sign up to receive emails from the seller in question. Again, this is a more difficult way to earn a commission, because it requires the consumer to do something that is largely out of your control. If you provide an incentive in your own way, this might make it easier to make money from this tactic.

26.   Type 4: Cost Per Action

27.   When you're involved in a program that is cost per action, this means that you're only going to get paid when the consumer completes some predefined action for which the seller is looking. For example, this may mean that you only get paid when the consumer downloads a specific item from the seller's site, or when the consumer completes a survey.

28.   These are the basic types of affiliate marketing programs that are out there. Make sure that you choose to work with a seller who offers the program in which you're most interested, and try not to compromise on what you want until it becomes clear that your options are limited. It's also important that you correspond with many sellers, to get an idea of the types of offers that are out there. Once you find a program, the seller will provide you with programming code that you can embed into your website. **Chapter 4:**

Amazon's Affiliate Marketing

Program

29. Amazon's affiliate marketing program, Amazon Associates, is arguably the most popular one on the internet today. Obviously, Amazon is an online marketplace powerhouse that provides millions of products to people all over the world. While you can certainly target smaller businesses when you're looking for products to promote, avoiding Amazon's marketplace would be silly because of its size and capacity for future growth. Below are the steps that you needs to take if you want your website to feature Amazon products.

30. **Step 1:** Set up your own website to make it ideal for selling affiliate products

31. **Step 2:**. If you want your affiliate account to be separate from your current Amazon account, create a new login prior to continuing. You'll find the "Amazon Associates" link on the menu page for your traditional Amazon account.

32. **Step 3:** Once you're in the Amazon Associates portal, click "Join for Free". Next, click "New Customer" and create an Associates account for yourself.

33. **Step 4:** Fill out the remainder of the application. This step is pretty similar to applying for any type of service. You'll be required to include your address and contact information. You'll also have to provide your website for review. Amazon wants to make sure that the work that you're already doing on your site will coincide nicely with the products that are available on Amazon. Make sure that you have some content on your website. If your site is empty, Amazon is not going to accept it.

34. **Step 5:** Wait for Amazon approval. Once Amazon approves your website, you'll be provided with links that you can embed into your posts and these will lead directly to the Amazon website.

35. That's it! It's pretty simple to get started with affiliate marketing through Amazon Associates, right?

36. Chapter 5: Common Mistakes to Avoid

37.   Now that you're aware of the basic concepts surrounding affiliate marketing and have tips to get started, let's take a look at some common mistakes that new affiliate marketers often make. This way, you'll be less likely to make these same mistakes yourself.

38.   Mistake 1: Failure to Cultivate an Email List

39.   If you can promote affiliate products through two platforms, why wouldn't you? You should strongly consider adding a contact page to your website so that you can begin to gather email addresses whenever you can. This way, you can supplement your website's affiliate marketing tactics with email marketing tactics as well.

40.   Mistake 2: Writing Inadequate Reviews

41.   From the perspective of SEO, it's commonly understood that most posts on any reputable website should be at least 2,000 words long. If they're not, it's almost guaranteed that you're going to rank lower on any search engine. Additionally, SEO can also sift through websites and see whether the content is made of quality material or garbage. It's important to take the time that's necessary to write practical and useful articles that will help consumers rather than confuse or frustrate them.

42. Mistake 3: Not Spending Enough Time Doing Research

43.   The importance of doing keyword research prior to

committing to a certain topic cannot be overstated. So many new affiliate marketing enthusiasts disregard the importance of doing sound keyword research prior to developing their site, and this results in utter and complete website failure. If you're not diligent during the research period, you're not going to be able to find a keyword that has a high search volume but low competition. Finding your niche is arguably the most important aspect of developing an affiliate marketing website.

44. **Mistake 4: Forgetting the Importance of Patience**

45. Creating a successful affiliate marketing website requires a lot of patience and dedication. If you're someone who tends to get irritated easily at obstacles, then you're going to want to adjust this attitude prior to starting your affiliate marketing pursuit. Google alone has over 200 credentials that they consider when ranking web pages for SEO, and it's hard to keep track of them all. Google does not publicly state what their SEO principles are, which is why you will have to be patient when figuring out what is going to work for your individual site. Be prepared to go through some periods of trial-and-error, and remember the importance of patience.

46.

47.

48.

49.

50.

51.

52. PART 3

53.

54.

55.

56.

57.

58.

59.

60. Chapter 1: Understanding Network Marketing

61. Before we get into how you can optimize a career for yourself in network marketing, we must first begin by fully understanding what network marketing is all about. Specifically, this chapter is going to focus on the topics of lead generation, recruiting and how to train the recruits that you eventually choose. It will also discuss the different types of network marketing hierarchies that exist, so that you will be able to figure out the type of structure that a company works within once you begin to look for network marketing work. All of these topics are essential when seeking to understand how network marketing functions, and without being informed about these topics the rest of the book will make less sense.

62. What is Network Marketing?

63. Network marketing is also known as multi-level marketing. This type of marketing can be best defined as a type of marketing strategy that is multi-tiered and often hierarchal in nature. Typically, a larger company or corporation will incentivize individuals to sell products on the company's behalf. In exchange for the salesman or saleswoman's time, the company will provide them with a commissioned percentage of their total sales. In other words, the corporation will provide the individual with the product to sell, and the individual will then be responsible for selling the products. Some examples of popular network marketing companies that you may have heard of include Mary Kay, Omnilife, and Rodan and Fields.

64. How Does It Work?

65. A network marketing business should not be too difficult to understand. If you come across one that is difficult to understand, you should be weary because there is a chance that it could be a front for some type of scam.

Typically, once you decide on the company for whom you want to work, you will be required to pay a small fee. This fee will usually not be more than a few hundred dollars. In exchange for your money, the company in question will provide you with a sample set of products that you can then sell to family, friends, or clients. If you decide to stick with the network marketing company after this trial period, you will still be paying the company so that you can sell the products that they're giving you, but the hope of any network marketing salesperson is to sell enough product to cover the cost of the product itself and also make a profit.

66. Often, an additional incentive that a network marketing company will put on an individual salesperson is the incentive to recruit other members who can work underneath of (you), the original salesperson. When you recruit more people to work underneath of you, you're provided with additional payment from the company who owns the rights to the product, and you're also paid when these salespeople make money as well. As you can see, this structure is hierarchal, with the product company being at the top and the people who are working underneath people like you at the bottom. You may start as a person who is low on the hierarchy, but the goal for a serious network marketer is to eventually become the middle manager who is recruiting people to work sales.

67. The Three Elements of Network Marketing

68. Typically, once you are involved with a network marketing company, there are going to be three elements of the business of which you should be aware. These elements include the notions of lead generation, recruiting methods, and adequately training your new recruits. Let's look at each of these elements separately:

69. Lead Generation: Lead generation is an essential aspect of any successful network marketer. If you don't start your network marketing career with a lot of leads, then it will be less likely that you will make a lot of sales. A great tactic to use when you're first starting out is to turn to the internet. Establishing a good online presence as a network marketer will be the subject of a subsequent chapter.

70. Recruiting Methods: Good recruiting methods are also important for any aspiring network marketer. While you may be the low man (or woman) on the totem pole when you're first starting out in a reputable network marketing company, you're only going to start making real money once you are recruiting your own sales people who can generate commissions on their sales for you. A great way to recruit people for sales is to talk to people who are interested in selling about the *results* of your own sales and the perks of working for the company.

71. Recruit Training: Once you have found people who are interested in working under you, you have to know how to train them properly. Otherwise, you will be managing people for free because they will not be making any money for you! An important aspect of training involves you taking on the role of mentor or coach for these new salespeople. You are going to want these people to feel as if they can rely on you for support when they need it, along with encouragement along the way. Without this support on your end and the ability to provide these people with strong direction, these people will be more likely to find work elsewhere.

72. **Single-Level Versus Multi-Level Marketing**

73. Lastly, it's important to understand how multi-level marketing differs from single-level marketing. It's safe to say that if you're looking to be as profitable as possible, you are going to gravitate towards multi-level marketing. With single-level marketing, you are still going to purchase product from a larger company, but you are not going to have anyone working underneath of you. This is the key difference between single-level marketing and multi-level marketing. As an aspiring network marketer, you may start out as single-level, but your ultimate goal (if you're serious), is to work towards being a multi-level marketer with employees who you manage, motivate, and from whom you receive a commissioned profit.

74.

75. Chapter 2: Tips on How to Find Network Marketing Success

76. Now that you have an understanding of what network marketing is and the basic concepts guiding this professional niche, it's time to look at some key tips that will help you get started on a successful path as quickly as possible. Without understanding and implementing the tips that are presented in this chapter, your initial sales are likely to be lower than they should be, and this will deter you from continuing with this potentially lucrative business. Additionally, these tips will help you to feel more confident as you move forward in your pursuit of becoming a successful network marketing agent.

77. Tip 1: Choose the Company You Want to Work for Carefully

78. It's likely that you've heard about how pyramid schemes can be disguised as legitimate network marketing businesses. Without getting into the details of a pyramid scheme, they are a way to deceitfully take people's money and you definitely do not want to become part of one. This is why it's extremely important that you choose a network marketing company to work for that you know is reputable and will be able to provide you with lucrative results. Here are some great things to research about the company, prior to committing yourself to it:

79. 1. Has the company been around for at least five years? Most network marketing firms fail within two years of being open. If you can find one that's been in business for at least five years, it's a sign that you may have found a good one.

80. 2. Is the company well-funded? A good piece of advice is to look to work for a company that is publicly traded on the stock market, because this means that they are required to publicly disclose how much money they're worth. You want to make sure that you're working for a company that can pay your commissions and provide you with great incentives (like the notorious Mary Kay pink Cadillac!).

81. 3. Does the company offer a unique service or product? You don't want to be trying to sell something that no one feels like they need in their lives. Before committing to a company, it'd be a good idea to make sure that this same type of product is not available somewhere else for a discount, and that there is not a ton of competition within the market for this particular product.

82. Tip 2: Analyze the Mentorship within the Program

83. In any type of network marketing program, the more experienced leaders within the program should be willing to help any newbie out via mentoring for at least thirty days. You want to make sure that this type of mentoring is in fact occurring within the network marketing company in which you choose to partake. Otherwise, it's likely that you will end up feeling lost, insecure, and unsuccessful. Within the industry, when a new member of group is not care for, it's known as "orphaning". Don't let yourself be an orphan. Do adequate research of the company prior to committing to it, so that there is no way that this can happen to you.

84. **Tip 3: Hire an Accountant**

85. Even though you are going to technically be working for a large company, you will still be responsible for taking care of your own taxes and other types of financial filings. Remember, you are going to get paid on commission most likely, and this means that you may have to provide invoices to the company that document the sales that you've made. Especially within the first year of being in business, you're going to want to make sure that you're doing everything right from the perspective of the government. Unless you have a background in accounting, you should do yourself a favor and hire someone who can assist you in these types of matters. These days, you may not even have to hire someone, and can instead look into accounting software for yourself.

86. **Tip 4: Be Hesitant to Quit Your Day Job**

87. Even though it's likely that you're interested in network marketing because it will provide you with flexible working hours, this does not mean that you should eagerly quit your full-time job as soon as you start working for the network marketing company. These networks take time to grow and take hold, and you don't want to be desolate as you work towards developing income in this new and exciting field. Once you start to make more money, you'll be given a better idea of how much you can expect to make through these means. It's only when you're confident that you can make a living wage that you should quit your current job to pursue network marketing to the fullest extent possible; unless of course, you have a spouse or someone else who has agreed to support you during this period of time.

88.

89.

90.

91.

92.

93.

94. Chapter 3: Successful Network Marketing Strategies and How to Find Your Audience

95. Now that we've gone over some tips that you should be thinking about when you're first getting started in network marketing, we are now going to turn our attention to the next step in this progression towards overall network marketing success. This chapter is going to be focusing on some of the key tactics that you can implement once you've chosen a company and are ready to really start going after clients to make money. Being in the network marketing business means that you're essentially a highly visible salesperson. This being the case, you want to make sure that your sales platforms are all planned carefully, smartly, and in a way that will yield real results.

96. Planning Your Approach

97. While the internet is certainly going to help your sales outreach, you're also going to want to take some time to truly figure out how much money you plan on making and how you can reach this point. One of the first questions that you should be able to succinctly answer prior to making a single sale is what type of business do you want this to be? Are you looking to make network marketing only a gig for yourself, or are you looking to recruit others and eventually make a small piece of an empire your own? It's generally recommended that if you're looking to make network marketing a part-time gig, you should be willing to devote between 3 to 10 hours of your time per week to the business. On the other hand, if know that you want to recruit people and eventually manage a small network yourself, expect to devote at least 15 hours a week to this venture. Knowing this information up front will help you to plan your weeks accordingly.

98. Additionally, you're going to want to take advantage of any training that the product's company can provide you. Most network marketing companies, if they're legitimate, will typically offer trainings and seminars to their salespeople. These meetings can take place over the internet or in person, and you should try to attend as many as you can. Not only will this help you financially if these trainings are paid, but they will also allow you to potentially meet mentors within the group and network with other people who are in your same position as a beginner. Networking is an extremely important aspect of this type of marketing structure. As you work through planning your approach, a good piece of advice to keep in mind is that you can never spend too much time attending promotional and informational events that are related to the product that you're selling.

99. Your Online Presence

100. These days, the internet is a powerful tool that any business should be using. This fact is no different for someone who is interested in network marketing. Let's take a look at some of the ways that you can easily gain exposure via an online platform.

101. Contact Reputable Blogs

102. You may or may not be aware of the fact that successful bloggers are also people who are constantly trying to make money through their writing. A primary way that a blogger is able to make money is through advertising. Wouldn't it be fabulous if a blogger could advertise your product for you to their own audience? Of course, the blogger will charge you a small fee in exchange for this service, but the upside to this fact is that you can arrange to only pay the blogger when a sale is made through their website. Some bloggers will want to review your product on their site and hope that this generates some interest, while others will simply want to advertise the product on their site and wait for people to buy it. Either way, this is free exposure and will allow you to gain an audience that would otherwise be inaccessible. Partaking in this type of venture also takes relatively little work on your part. All you have to do is reach out to a bunch of blogs and see if any of them are interested in working with you.

103.   Activate the Powers of Social Media

104.   Once you start selling product, it would be smart to set up social media accounts for your product as well. Once your accounts are up and running, you should also set a schedule for yourself to follow in regards to your posting frequency. Here is a list of the types of accounts you should consider setting up, along with a good schedule to follow:

Account Type	Posting Frequency
Twitter	At least 3 times per day, if not more
Facebook	No more than twice per day
Google+	No more than three times per day
LinkedIn	Once per day

105.   If you think that you may not be able to keep track of a social media schedule on your own, there are plenty of free social media scheduling tools that exist on the web. A great one to consider is MassPlanner. This tool will allow you to consolidate your social media posting calendar in one easily accessible place. In order for this type of tactic to work for you, make sure that you're looking at the people who are liking and sharing your content. These are the types of people who are going to be most useful to you from a targeting perspective. Don't let these people get away! Follow up with them in some manner.

106. **Narrowing in On Your Target Audience**

107. For any type of marketing, it's extremely important to understand that your audience is *not* everyone. This is an essential concept to understand, especially for the type of marketing that we're discussing. As a marketing professional, one of your jobs needs to be narrowing in on your target audience, rather than simply advertising to everyone and hoping that the people who are interested will find what you're selling. The reality is that advertisements are everywhere in our society. You don't want the product that you're selling to get lost in the shuffle. Below are a few questions that you should ask yourself that will help you to narrow in on who it is you should be looking for when you are attempting to sell your product:

1. **What problem does my product solve for people?** Present your product as a *solution* to this particular problem that your audience is facing.

2. **Who are your current customers?** Because of the fact that the company for whom you're working should already have a solid client base, you should be able to figure out the types of people who are gravitating towards the product that you're selling with relative ease. You should consider asking the company's sales team or people who have been working for the company for a while for this type of information.

3. **What are the Unique Features of the Product that You're Selling?** How does your product differ from the product of

your competitor? These are the features that you should be emphasizing to your potential clients. Is there something that your product does that similar products don't? Tell your audience! These details are sure to set your product apart from the rest.

4.   This chapter has discussed ways that you can spend your time working towards network marketing success, both through physical means and digital means via the internet. Particularly with the online strategies that you can use for your sales practices, it's important to understand that neither of these approaches require that you develop a website of your own. Of course, you can certainly develop one if you wish to do so, but developing a website is often a time consuming and costly matter. This book seeks to offer strategies that are of the lowest possible cost to you, both from the perspective of your finances and time.

5.

6. Chapter 4: Common Mistakes that New Network Marketers Make and How to Avoid Them

7.   Now that you're fully aware of top tips to follow when network marketing and have also been given some concrete strategies that you can implement to find success, we will now turn our attention to the topic of mistakes that other network marketers commonly make. This may seem like a pessimistic topic to cover, but the reality is that if you are aware of these types of mistakes, there is less of a chance that you will make them yourself. With knowledge of these mistakes under your belt, you'll be in a much better position from an educational perspective, and this knowledge will be able to healthily influence your decisions in the future.

8.   **Common Mistake 1: Choosing to work for a company that focuses on recruiting more than it does sales generation**

9.   You need to make sure that you're choosing to work for a network marketing company that is focusing on the generation of new sales, rather than trying to primarily motivate you to recruit new people. If the company is not focusing the majority of its energy on selling the product, then

how do you expect to ever make real money? This is a major problem that many newbie network marketers seem to miss. Don't allow yourself to be one of them!

10. **Common Mistake 2: Targeting Friends and Family to No End**

11. Obviously, when you're first starting out in the network marketing field, it can be tricky to find leads that are not members of your friends or family. Some coaching books and other forms of network marketing advice will tell you to make a list of 100 friends and family members who you can use as sources of lead generation when you're first starting, but this is not usually good advice. You want to push yourself to try to find legitimate leads, rather than pester your family and friends relentlessly. The harder that you work at finding true leads, the easier time you will have establishing real connections with people who are truly interested in your product over the long-term.

12. **Common Mistake 3: Selling to your recruits, rather than attracting them**

13. With network marketing, a key aspect of being successful is finding salespeople who are eager to work underneath of you; however, you need to be careful about how you attract these people. Many beginners will try and coerce people into becoming a seller underneath of them, instead of sitting back and attracting the people who are truly interested in this type of endeavor. When you sell to someone who is not truly a

good fit for this type of work, you are setting both yourself and the person in question up for failure. You may find yourself making promises to this person that you will ultimately be unable to keep, and this person may also be someone who is going to only cause you headaches later on down the line. Be sure to find sellers who are going to work well with you, so that you can avoid unnecessary problems in the future.

14. Common Mistake 4: You fail to get out there and sell

15. Even though this book discussed strategies that could be used on the internet, those tactics were not meant to replace the person-to-person tactics that you should be implementing from the jump. Remember, a key aspect of this type of marketing can be found in the name itself. If you do not network properly and constantly push yourself to attend as many events as you can, it is much less likely that you will end up seeing the sales numbers that you hope to anticipate.

16. Common Mistake 5: Talking negatively to the people working under you

17. It's important to remember that the people who are working under you should not be considered your friends. They are your employees, and their job is to make you a percentage of money every time that they make a sale. So often, people who are new to network marketing tend to consider their salespeople as friends. As the leader of this group, it's your job to constantly motivate your team to success. If instead of motivating, you're spending your time talking negatively about the company as a whole or about clients who are purchasing your product, you are setting a negative tone for the entire operation.

18. To rectify this type of problem, it is always a better idea to go to someone who is higher up on the chain than you are. Not only will this allow you to be perceived more positively by your sellers; it will also more likely lead to a sound solution to any problems that you may be having. Remember, you are in charge! It's important that you act like a leader. Otherwise, the negativity that you portray could begin to negatively influence the number of sales that you're generating, because your sales team feels discouraged and unsure. Be the approachable person you'd want your own boss to be, and you won't go wrong.

19.

20.

21.

22.

23.

24.

25.

26.

27.

28.

29.

30. THANK YOU

31.

32. Dear treasured reader, I would like to thank you from the bottom of my heart for choosing to purchase this book. I hope you've gotten some valuable information that you can use right now to build a successful online business for yourself. I would appreciate it very much.

In case you missed it earlier, if you would like to receive latest tips and tricks on internet marketing, exclusive strategies, upcoming books & promotions, and **more,** do subscribe to my mailing list in the link below! I will be giving away a free book that you can download *right away* as well after you subscribe to show my appreciation!

Here's the link: http://bit.do/jonathanswalker

33.

34.

Once again thank you and all the best to your success!

Jonathan S. Walker

35.

36.

37. About The Author
38.

39.

40. Hi there it's Jonathan Walker here, I want to share a little bit about myself so that we can get to know each other on a deeper level. I grew up in California, USA, and have lived there for the better part of my life. Being exposed to many different people and opportunities when I was young, it made me want to strive to become an entrepreneur to escape the rat race path that most of my peers had taken. I knew I wanted to be able to travel and experience the world the way it was meant to be seen and I've done just that. I've travelled to most places around the world and I'm enjoying every minute of it for sure. In my free time I love to play tennis and believe it or not, compose songs. I wish you all the best again in your endeavours, and may your dreams, whatever they may be, come true abundantly in the near future.

41.

42.

43.

44.